Super-Duper Science

Peculiar Plants!

by Annalisa McMorrow

illustrated by Marilynn G. Barr

For Susie

Publisher: Roberta Suid
Design & Production: Scott McMorrow
Cover Design: David Hale
Cover Art: Mike Artell
Copy Editor: Carol Whiteley
Educational Consultant: Tanya Lieberman

Also by the author: *Save the Animals!* (MM1964), *Love the Earth!* (MM1965), *Learn to Recycle!* (MM1966), *Sing a Song About Animals* (MM1987), *Preschool Connections* (MM1993), *Incredible Insects! (and Spiders, Too)* (MM2018), *Spectacular Space!* (MM2019), *Outstanding Oceans!* (MM2020), *Ladybug, Ladybug* (MM2015), *Twinkle, Twinkle* (MM2016), *Rub-a-Dub-Dub* (MM2017), *Daffy-Down-Dilly* (MM2037), *Pussycat, Pussycat* (MM2036), *Rain, Rain, Go Away!* (MM2038), *Amazing Animals!* (MM2059), and *Wacky Weather!* (MM2057).

Entire contents copyright © 1998 by
Monday Morning Books, Inc.
For a complete catalog, please write to the address below:

P.O. Box 1680, Palo Alto, CA 94302 U.S.A.

Call us at: 1-800-255-6049

E-mail us at: MMBooks@aol.com

Visit our Web site:
http://www.mondaymorningbooks.com

Monday Morning Books is a registered trademark of
Monday Morning Books, Inc.

ISBN 1-57612-044-9

Printed in the United States of America
987654321

Contents

Introduction: Why Plants?

Plants can be giant (the rafflesia of Sumatra has a flower that weighs 15 lbs./7 kg.), explosive (Scotch broom flowers explode open when a bee lands on them), tricky (carnivorous plants bait and trap animals for food), and all-around peculiar!

Children will learn about the exciting plant world while practicing writing, reading, research, performance, and speaking skills. They'll learn how plants grow, give fairy ring reports, weigh a coconut, learn about "walking" trees, star in a musical review, and much more. Most of the activities can easily be simplified for younger children or extended for upper grades. This book will enhance learning in many subjects through exploration of the plants in our world.

Peculiar Plants! is divided into four parts (plus a resource section). **Hands-On Discoveries** contains activities that allow children to participate in answering science questions they may have, for example, "How do Venus flytraps work?" or "How do cacti drink?" Reproducible sheets have information or directions written specifically for the children. These sheets are marked with a special leaf icon.

Nonfiction Book Links features speaking, writing, and reporting activities based on nonfiction resources. Most activities are accompanied by helpful handouts that lead children through the research procedure. When research is required, you have the option of letting children look for the facts needed in the library (or in books you've checked out ahead of time). Or they may use the "Super-Duper Fact Cards" located in the resource section at the back of this book. These cards list information for 16 unusual plants. Duplicate the cards onto neon-colored paper, and cut them out. Laminate the cards, and cut them out again, making sure to leave a thin laminate border to prevent peeling. Keep the cards in a box for children to choose from when doing their research. These cards also provide an opportunity for younger children to do research by giving them needed information in a simple, easy-to-understand format.

The **Fiction Book Links** section uses storybooks and chapter books to introduce information about interesting types of plants, such as the ones in *The Garden of Abdul Gasazi*. This section's activities, projects, and language extensions help children connect with both real and fictional plants. Each "Link" also includes a tongue twister. You can challenge children to create their own twisters from the plant facts they've learned. Also included in this section are decorating suggestions for "setting the stage" for each particular book.

It's Show Time! presents new songs sung to old tunes, and costume suggestions for putting on a performance. The songs can be duplicated and given to the children. If you want to hold a performance, write each performer's name on the reproducible program page and give copies to your audience.

Each of the first three sections ends with a "Super-Duper Project," an activity that uses the information children have learned in the unit. These projects include building tricky traps (similar to the carnivorous Venus flytrap), creating a fact tree forest, and writing new plant fables. A choral performance is a possible "Super-Duper" ending for the "It's Show Time!" section.

The last two pages of the book are nonfiction resources to share with children, and plant-related Web sites to explore.

Suggestions for Extending Lessons:
• Invite a representative from a nursery to speak to your children.
• Have children observe plant life around them.
• Go on a field trip to a botanical garden, a greenhouse, or a neighborhood park.
• Grow flowers in a window box or start a simple herb garden.
• Grow an avocado tree: suspend the pit, large end down, with toothpicks over a water-filled glass. When roots are thick, plant in soil with half the seed exposed.

All About Plants

Most plants are fixed in one place. Green plants make their own food. These plants contain chlorophyll. They give off oxygen, which people and animals breathe. Plants provide oxygen for our atmosphere. Without green plants, there wouldn't be enough oxygen in the air for people to survive. Let's thank the plants!

Some plants, called fungi, do not make their own food. Mushrooms fall into this category. Some mushrooms are so tiny, you need a magnifying glass to see them. These mushrooms grow in moss or on old logs. Other mushrooms can weigh up to 20 lbs./9 kg. each. They spend the first two weeks of their lives growing underground, before popping out of the ground.

Flowers use their colors and scents to attract insects. Bees and butterflies are attracted by brightly colored flowers and by the flowers' scents.

A tree is a tall plant with a single woody stem. There are two main groups of trees: deciduous and evergreen. Deciduous trees lose their leaves in the fall. Oaks, beeches, and maples are deciduous trees. Most deciduous trees have broad leaves. Pines, cypress trees, and spruce trees are evergreens. They stay green all year round. Most evergreen trees have cones instead of flowers. Palm trees have characteristics that fit into both categories.

Plants and Seeds

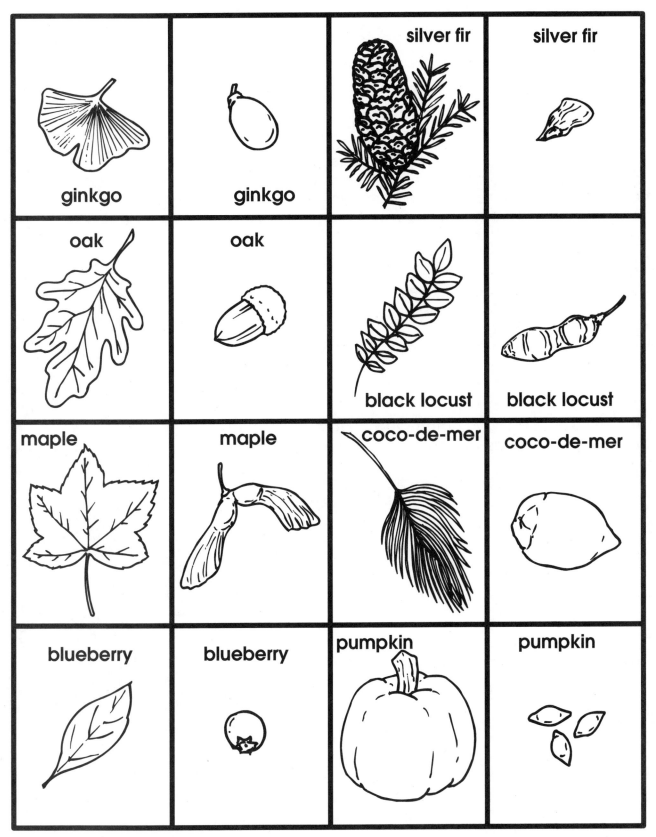

ginkgo

ginkgo

silver fir

silver fir

oak

oak

black locust

black locust

maple

maple

coco-de-mer

coco-de-mer

blueberry

blueberry

pumpkin

pumpkin

Serve a Salad

Materials:
Drawing paper, crayons or markers

Directions:
1. Explain that different parts of a plant have different names: leaves, stalks, flowers, roots, and so on.
2. Ask children if they've ever eaten flowers. Continue through the rest of the parts of the plant, having children raise their hands if they've eaten each part.
3. Give each child a sheet of drawing paper and crayons or markers. Have the children draw a salad and label the parts of the plants that are used. For example, broccoli and cauliflower are the flowers of plants. Celery is a stalk. Lettuce is a leaf. Carrots and radishes are roots. Challenge children to draw salads that contain all the parts of a plant (flowers, root, stem or stalk, and leaf).
4. Post the completed pictures on a "Super Salad" bulletin board.

Options:
• Ask if any children have eaten seeds before. Discuss edible seeds: sunflower seeds, pumpkin seeds, corn kernels, poppy seeds, and so on.
• Bring in real vegetables and challenge children to make a salad with all parts of a plant: stalk, flower, leaf, roots.

Glow Plants

Some plants give off light. They glow in the daytime and at night, but they're only visible in the dark. Glowing plants shine with a green light, orange light, or yellow light. Many mushrooms glow. And many plants that live at the bottom of the ocean glow, too.

Materials:
Black or blue construction paper, hole punch, clear cellophane (yellow, green, and orange), tape or glue, light-colored crayons

Directions:
1. Give each child a sheet of colored construction paper.
2. Have the children color the paper using light-colored crayons. They can draw mushrooms, or they can use their imaginations to draw the types of plants that grow under water.
3. Provide hole punches for children to use to punch holes in their plants and mushrooms.
4. Provide different colors of clear cellophane for children to glue or tape to the backs of their pictures.
5. Post the pictures on a window that gets plenty of sunlight.
6. Turn out the lights in the classroom and close the curtains except for the parts of the windows that have the pictures on them.
7. Have children observe their glowing plants.

Fun Fact:
Some people call plants' light "foxfire."

Concerning Cacti

The saguaro (sa-WAH-ro) cactus is the largest cactus in the world. Sometimes it grows to be 50 ft. (30 m.) tall. The saguaro can bloom and grow fruit for years with almost no rain. Some saguaros drink so much that they burst!

Materials:
"Crazy Cacti" Hands-on Handout (p. 11), paper, pencils, measuring cups, different-sized containers (bottles, milk cartons, or cans)

Directions:
1. Discuss the fact that saguaros can go for a long time without water. When there is water, they drink as much as they can.
2. Divide the children into groups of four or five. Duplicate the "Crazy Cacti" Hands-on Handout for groups to observe.
3. Give each group a piece of paper, a pencil, a container, and a set of measuring cups.
4. Have the groups guess how much water their container can hold.
5. Take the children outside and have them use the measuring cups to fill their containers. They should keep track of how much water it takes to fill the containers. If the children guess incorrectly, their containers will either overflow or be partly empty.
6. Have children record whether their guesses were close, correct, or too much. Then have them empty the water from the containers. (Try to find plants that need water, so there will be little waste.)

Note:
This can be a wet activity!

Peculiar Plants! © 1998 Monday Morning Books, Inc.

Crazy Cacti

The **Rat's Tail Cactus** hangs from tree branches or rocks in the wild. It does not bloom at all until it is five years old.

The **Old Man Cactus** grows slowly. It has spines that look like long white hairs.

The **Fire Crown Cactus** is small and round. The flowers grow from the sides of the stems. The flowers open in the mornings and close in the evenings.

The **Orange Cob Cactus** has flowers that bloom on tubes growing from its sides. These flowers open in the evening.

Mangrove Mural

Each of the mangrove's seeds grows a root while it's still attached to the tree. The seed drops off the tree and into the water. Sometimes the seed floats away, but sometimes it starts growing right next to the parent tree. Sand and dirt get trapped in the roots and this builds up an island of mangroves. The trees never stop spreading, which is why they're called "walking trees."

Materials:
"Super-Duper Fact Card" on mangroves (p. 72), butcher paper, tempera paint (green, blue, brown), shallow tins, paintbrushes

Directions:
1. Discuss how a mangrove tree grows. Share the facts listed above and on the "Super-Duper Fact Card."
2. Provide a large sheet of butcher paper and shallow tins of green, blue, and brown tempera paint.
3. Have children work together to paint an island of mangrove trees. Start them off by drawing one mangrove tree in the center of the mural.
4. Have each child pretend to be a seed that's dropped off the tree into the water. The children should draw spidery roots coming out of the water and into new trees. Then they can draw new trees from these trees, and so on, until the butcher paper is filled.
5. Post the "Mangrove Mural" in a hallway or in the classroom along with a fact sheet about mangrove trees.

Peculiar Plants! © 1998 Monday Morning Books, Inc.

Loco for Coconuts

One palm tree, called the coco-de-mer, has a seed that can weigh up to 45 lbs./20 kg. This is about the weight of a kindergartner. This makes it the largest seed of any plant!

Materials:
"Plants and Seeds" sheet (p. 7), scale, variety of seeds (apple, orange, cherry, watermelon, pumpkin), variety of items to weigh (phone books, dictionaries, and so on)

Directions:
1. Discuss the fact that each plant's seeds are different.
2. Give each child a copy of the "Plants and Seeds" sheet to observe.
3. Divide the children into small groups. Have them weigh different seeds and compare the weights.
4. Let them compare the weights of apple seeds, watermelon seeds, orange seeds, pumpkin seeds, and other small seed varieties with the weight of a coconut. Either bring in a coconut for children to weigh, or explain that the heaviest seed weighs up to 45 lbs./20 kg. and let children use phone books or other heavy items to build an equal weight on the scale.

Option:
Bring in a coconut for children to sample.

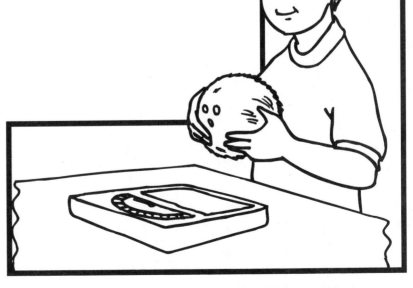

Peculiar Plants! © 1998 Monday Morning Books, Inc.

Apartment Trees

Trees can be homes to a wide variety of animals and insects. Sometimes you can see the creatures who live in a tree, such as squirrels and birds. Other times the tree's inhabitants are too small or too well camouflaged.

Materials:
"Tree Dweller Patterns" (p. 15), scissors, crayons or markers, construction paper or butcher paper, glue

Directions:
1. Discuss the different animals that might be found in the "litter" at the base of a tree: snails, caterpillars, toads, and earthworms. (Tree "litter" is made up of fallen and decaying leaves.)
2. Discuss the types of animals children might find in a tree: birds, squirrels, bats, bees (in a hive), moths, and so on.
3. Provide groups of four or five children with large sheets of construction paper or butcher paper. Have the children work together to draw large trees.
4. Duplicate a copy of the "Tree Dweller Patterns" for each group. Have the children color the patterns, cut them out, and glue them to their trees.
5. Post the trees on a "Friendly Forest" bulletin board.

Option:
Have children do research to find out one fact about trees. Post the facts on leaf-shaped pieces of paper attached to the trees.

Storybook Link:
• *The Great Kapok Tree: A Tale of the Amazon Rain Forest* by Lynne Cherry (Harcourt, 1990).

Tree Dweller Patterns

Ring of Roses

Materials:

"Ring o' Roses" Hands-on Handout (p. 17), tissue paper in assorted colors, scissors, egg cartons, pipe cleaners, glue, green construction paper (cut into leaf shapes), vases

Directions:

1. Duplicate the "Ring o' Roses" Hands-on Handout and use it to discuss different types of roses, including hybrid roses. Ask if any of the children has ever seen a rose. They may have seen them in botanical gardens or in yards in their neighborhoods.
2. Explain that when people create new flowers, they need to name them. Sometimes flowers are named for people. Sometimes flowers are named for the colors of their blossoms.
3. Provide assorted colors of tissue paper for children to use to make their own roses. They can gather cut pieces of tissue paper together and bind the pieces with pipe cleaner stems. Or they can glue tissue paper to egg carton sections and attach pipe cleaners to the sections.
4. While the roses dry, children can name their flowers. They can write the names on leaf-shaped pieces of paper and glue these to the pipe cleaner stems.
5. Gather the completed flowers and place them in vases, or in coffee cans that children decorate with layers of tissue paper.

Options:

• If children need help naming their flowers, write a list of adjectives on the board that they can use to describe their creations.
• Order a catalog from a garden company to share with the students. Often these catalogs have good examples of hybrid roses. Some popular roses include: Crimson Glory, Red Masterpiece, Taj Mahal, Summer Sunshine, Sunset Jubilee, Firelight, Fragrant Cloud, Candy Apple, Carrousel, Goldilocks, Portrait, Gypsy, Mojave, and Sterling Silver.
• Bring in a crayon box with a wide variety of crayon colors. Have children find the crayon colors that are named for flowers, fruits, and vegetables.

Ring o' Roses

Man-made roses are known as hybrids.

Hybrid plants are produced by breeding plants of different varieties.

Many thousands of roses have been produced in the past 150 years.

New roses appear each year. These flowers often have unique colors and descriptive names.

Peculiar Plants! © 1998 Monday Morning Books, Inc.

Tricky Traps

Carnivorous plants are plants that eat insects, small rodents, small water animals, and birds. Each plant has a different method of catching its prey. Explain to your students that there are no plants that eat people!

Materials:
"Bug-Eating Plants" Hands-on Handout (p. 19), paper plates, egg cartons, glue, scissors, construction paper, glitter glue (glue mixed with glitter and stored in squeeze bottles), pipe cleaners, felt, waxed paper

Directions:
1. Duplicate a copy of the "Bug-Eating Plants" Hands-on Handout for each child to observe.
2. After the children look at the different types of carnivorous plants, explain that they will be creating their own tricky traps.
3. Provide an assortment of arts and crafts materials for children to use to create their own versions of carnivorous plants. They can follow the methods used by the various plants (the trapdoors of the bladderworts, the open jaws of the Venus flytraps, the sticky flowers of the butterworts, or the deep holes of the jugs), or they can make up their own types of plants and methods.
4. Display the finished "Tricky Traps" on a table in your classroom or in the library. Place a few books about carnivorous plants on a table nearby.
5. Let children vote on the most unique, most frightening, most colorful (and so on) types of plants. (Make sure each plant wins an award.)

Option:
Duplicate the flies for children to glue to their tricky traps.

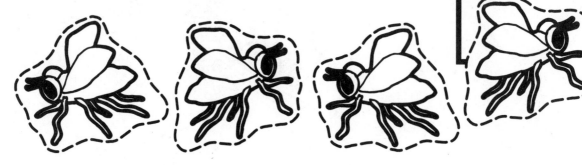

Peculiar Plants! © 1998 Monday Morning Books, Inc.

Bug-Eating Plants

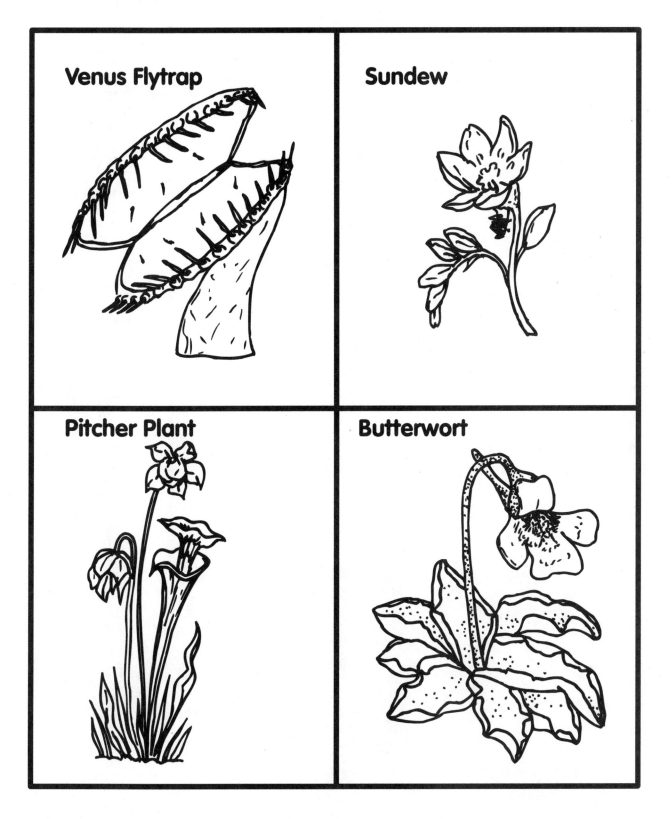

Venus Flytrap

Sundew

Pitcher Plant

Butterwort

The Biggest Tree

Sequoias are the largest living trees in the world. They can grow to be about 250 ft./76 m. tall. That's as tall as a 25-story building! The trunks can be over 30 ft./9 m. wide.

Materials:
Measuring tape, duct tape, string, scissors, chalk

Directions:
1. Tell the children they are going to find out how many children will fit in a sequoia tree.
2. Cut a piece of string 15 ft./4.5 m. long.
3. Attach the string to the ground firmly, using duct tape.
4. Tie a piece of chalk to the free end of the string.
5. Pull the string taut (gently) and walk in a circle, marking the circle with chalk.
6. This is the circumference of the giant sequoia. Have the children guess how many children will fit inside the circle. Test their hypotheses by having them stand inside the chalk outline. If you need to, invite other classes to join your experiment.

Note:
Make sure to keep tension on the string while you walk in the circle.

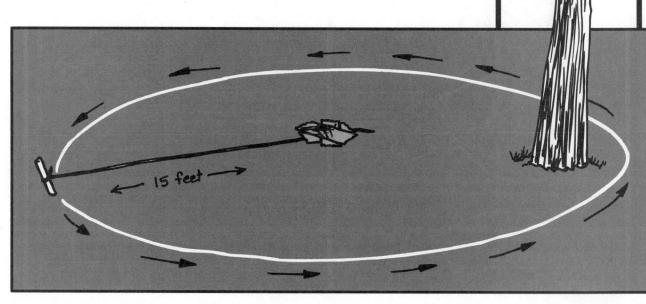

15 feet

Peculiar Plants! © 1998 Monday Morning Books, Inc.

Poison Ivy Game

Materials:
"Plant Playing Cards" (pp. 22–24), crayons or markers, scissors

Directions:
1. Make two copies of the "Plant Playing Cards," color, and cut apart. (Discard one Poison Ivy card.)
2. Laminate the playing cards and cut out again, leaving a thin, laminate border to prevent peeling.
3. Teach children how to play the game. The object is to collect the most pairs of plants without getting caught with the Poison Ivy card. (Children play the game like "Old Maid.")

How to Play the Game (2 to 4 players):
• Shuffle the cards and deal them, one at a time, face down to all players. It's okay for some players to have extra cards.
• Each player picks up his or her hand and sees if there are any pairs. All matched pairs should be placed on the table, face up.
• One child is chosen to start. He or she picks one card from the next player's hand (the player on the right).
• If the card drawn matches one in the first player's hand, the matched pair is placed face up on the table and the player picks again.
• If the card does not match, the new card is added to the player's hand and the next player takes a turn, choosing a card from the player on his or her right.
• The game continues until all pairs of cards are matched. The player with the most pairs is the winner. The player holding the Poison Ivy card is the loser.

Notes:
• Remind children to hold their hands so that the other players cannot see which cards they are picking.
• As the children make sets, they put them down. The child who has the most sets is the winner.

Option:
For younger children, make two copies of each card and let the children play Concentration.

Peculiar Plants! © 1998 Monday Morning Books, Inc.

Plant Playing Cards

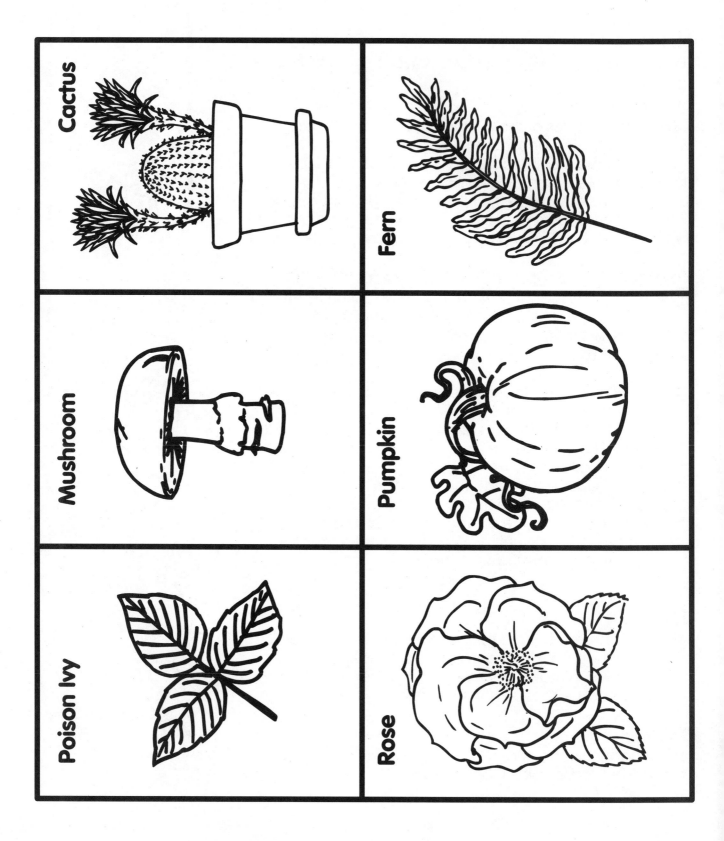

Plant Playing Cards

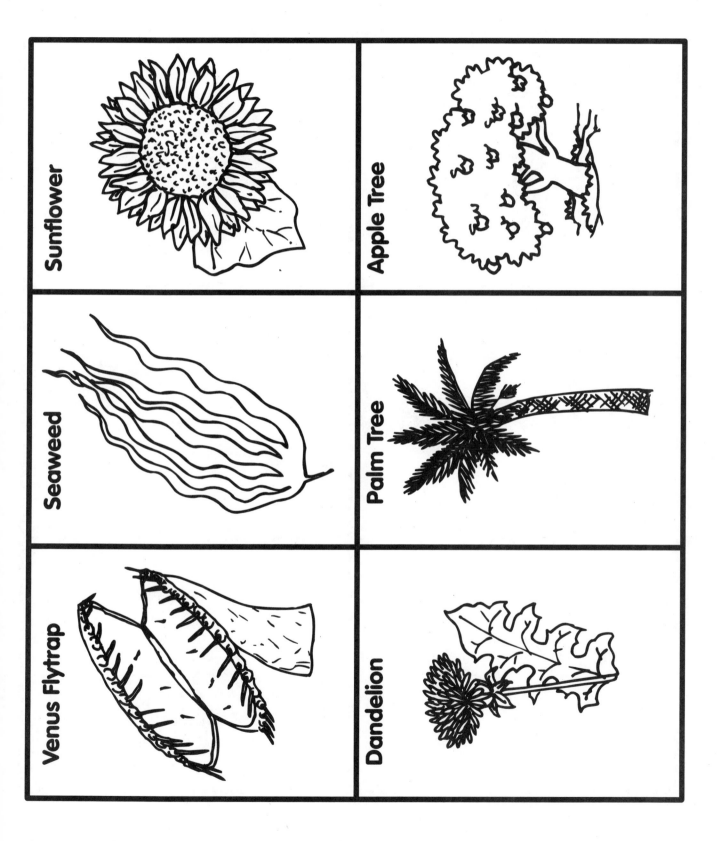

Plant Playing Cards

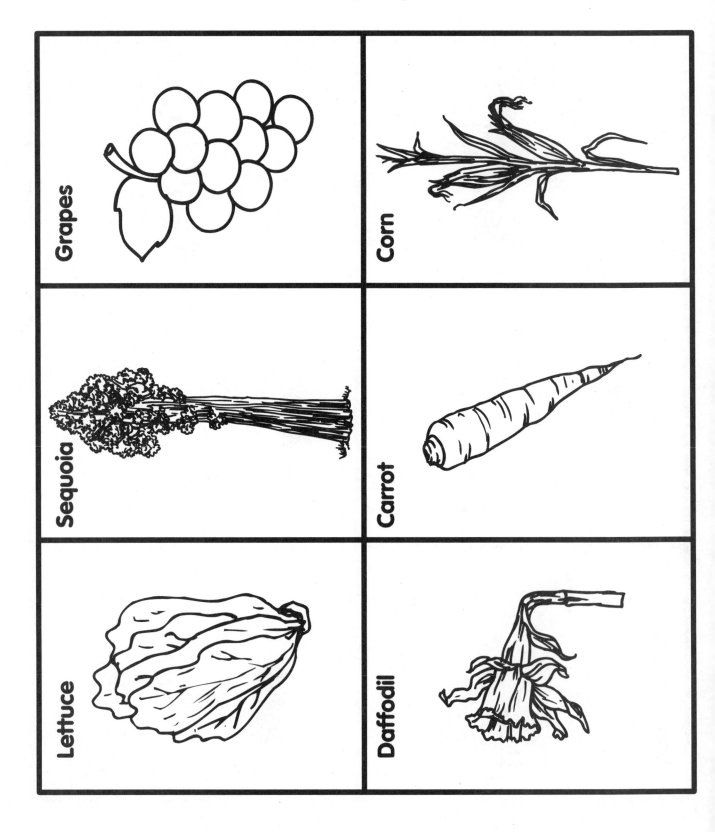

Magnificent Mushrooms

Many mushrooms have descriptive names as well as scientific names. For example, there is a mushroom called the chicken-of-the-woods and one known as squirrel's bread.

Materials:
"Marvelous Mushrooms" Hands-on Handout (p. 26), crayons or markers, scissors, construction paper

Directions:
1. Duplicate the "Marvelous Mushrooms" Hands-on Handout for children to observe.
2. Discuss the fact that although few vegetables have funny names, mushrooms are often given descriptive names, or nicknames.
3. Provide construction paper for children to use to draw their own mushrooms. They should make them as creative as possible.
4. Have children name their mushrooms.
5. Children should label the mushrooms and cut them out.
6. Post the mushrooms on a "Magnificent Mushrooms" bulletin board.

Options:
• Have a contest to see who can come up with the silliest mushroom. Or give each mushroom a special award: the most colorful, largest, smallest, scariest, and so on.
• Transcribe the names for younger students.
• Make mushrooms from spools, cupcake holders, corks, and so on. Or make colorful playdough mushrooms. Refer to the Resources section (p. 78) for the recipe.

Candy-Striped Mushroom

Tulip Mushroom

Double Gumdrop Mushroom

Polka-dot Bubble Mushroom

Peculiar Plants! © 1998 Monday Morning Books, Inc.

Marvelous Mushrooms

Golden Chanterelle

Morel

Deathcap

Earthstar

Elves' Saddle

Fairy Ring

Squirrel's Bread

Inky Cap

Fairy Cup

Plant Glossary

Materials:

"Plant Glossary" Hands-on Handouts (pp. 28–29), writing paper, pens or pencils, dictionaries, construction paper, stapler, glue, scissors

Directions:

1. Duplicate the glossary pages, making one sheet for each child. Explain that a glossary is a list of words with definitions.
2. Have children look up each word in the dictionary.
3. Children should write the definition next to the word to create their own plant glossaries. (Younger children can draw pictures.)
4. As children learn new plant words, have them add the words to their plant glossaries.
5. Provide construction paper and a stapler for children to use to bind their pages together. They can decorate the covers with pictures of plants.

Options:

• White-out the words in the leaves and duplicate one page for each child. Have children write in their own plant-related words and definitions.
• Let children decorate the covers of their books with dried leaves or flowers pressed between sheets of clear Contac paper.

Plant Glossary

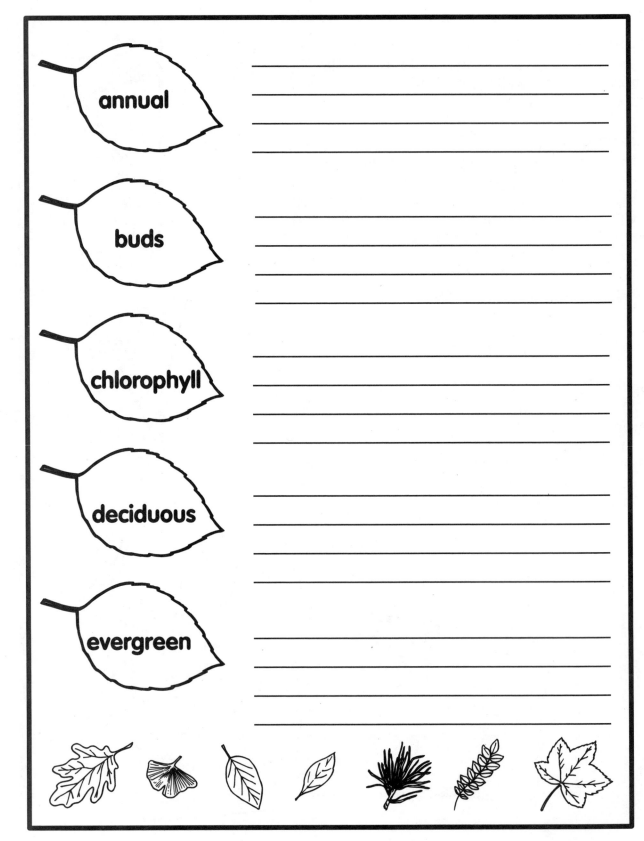

annual

buds

chlorophyll

deciduous

evergreen

Plant Glossary

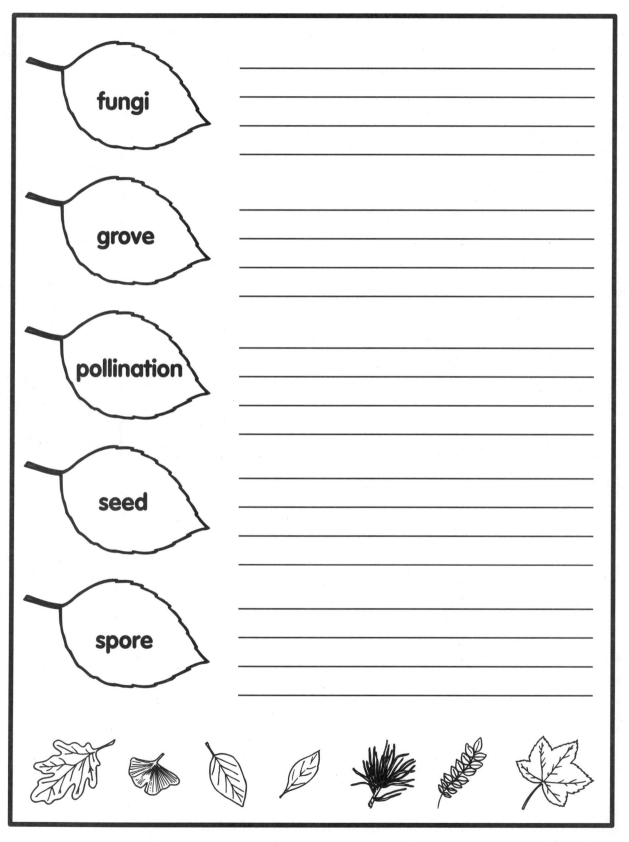

fungi

grove

pollination

seed

spore

Leaf Spelling

Materials:
"Spelling Leaf Patterns" (pp. 31–32), "Tree Pattern" (p. 33), scissors, crayons or markers, tape or glue

Directions:
1. Duplicate a copy of the "Spelling Leaf Patterns" for each child. Duplicate a few extra sheets for adult use.
2. Enlarge and duplicate the "Tree Pattern," color, and post on the bulletin board. Cut out one extra set of "leaves" and post them on the "Tree Pattern."
3. Have children learn the spelling of each word. They can pair off and test each other as a way of practicing.
4. Host a "Leaf Spelling" contest in your classroom. Keep one set of leaves in a hat and pull out one at a time, asking each child in turn to spell the word on the leaf.
5. Continue with the spelling contest, using the process of elimination. (Children who misspell a word sit down. The rest continue to try to spell the words.)

Note:
For additional spelling words, refer to the "Plant A to Z List" (p. 77).

Options:
• Duplicate blank spelling leaves, and let children write in their own plant-related words.
• Duplicate both the "Tree Pattern" and the leaves for younger children. They can simply glue or tape the leaves to the tree and practice tracing the words.

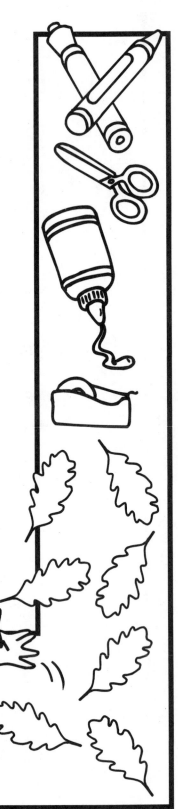

Peculiar Plants! © 1998 Monday Morning Books, Inc.

Spelling Leaf Patterns

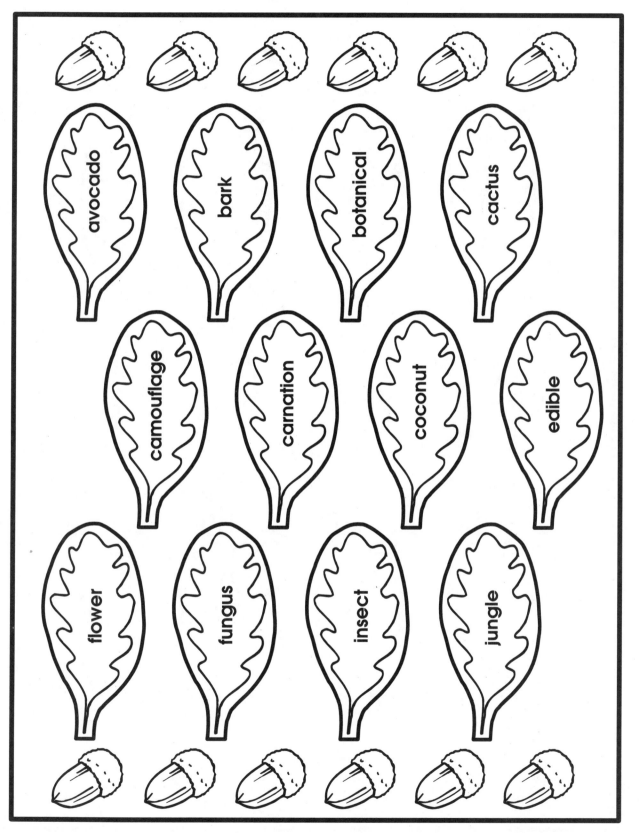

Spelling Leaf Patterns

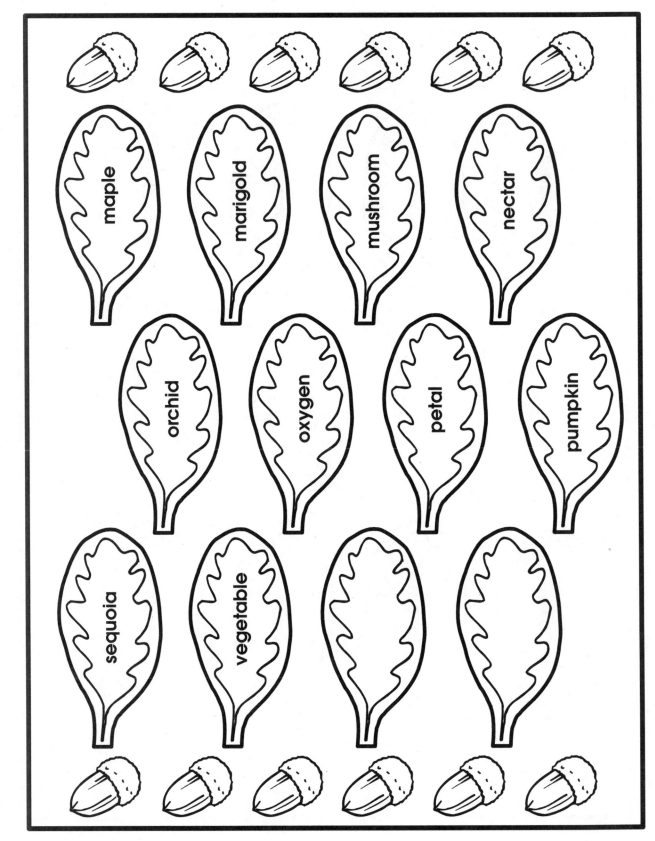

maple · marigold · mushroom · nectar · orchid · oxygen · petal · pumpkin · sequoia · vegetable

Tree Pattern

Interview a Plant

Materials:
"Super-Duper Fact Cards" (pp. 69–76), "Plant Fact Sheet" Hands-on Handout (p. 35), "Plant Interview Sheet" Hands-On Handout (p. 36), pencils or markers

Directions:
1. In these reports, children research plants and then play the part of their chosen plants in interview settings.
2. Let each child choose a plant from the "Super-Duper Fact Cards." Children can do research using the fact card. Or they can use books from the library.
3. Duplicate one copy of the "Plant Fact Sheet" Hands-on Handout and the "Plant Interview Sheet" Hands-on Handout for each child.
4. Have the children research their chosen plants using the guidelines on the "Plant Fact Sheet." Then have them write questions based on the facts using the "Plant Interview Sheet."
5. Once the children have finished their research, divide them into pairs. Have each partner take a turn interviewing the other in front of the class.
6. Set up an interview schedule, perhaps working through five to six interviews per day.

Note:
Children can also write reports on other plant-related topics. Have them choose from the "Plant A to Z List" (p. 77).

Options:
• Interviewers can hold simple microphones (cardboard tubes with egg carton sections glued to the top).
• Interviewees can also make simple costumes or masks to wear when they give their interviews.
• If you want to focus on specific types of plants, have children choose from fruits, vegetables, fungi, cacti, and so on.

Plant Fact Sheet

Use this fact sheet to record at least four facts about your chosen plant.
Remember to list the books you use.
You can use the back of this sheet if you need more room.

My name is:

_____

My plant is:

_____

Fact:

_____

Fact:

_____

Fact:

_____

Fact:

_____

Books I used:

_____

Title:

_____

Author:

_____

Title:

_____

Author:

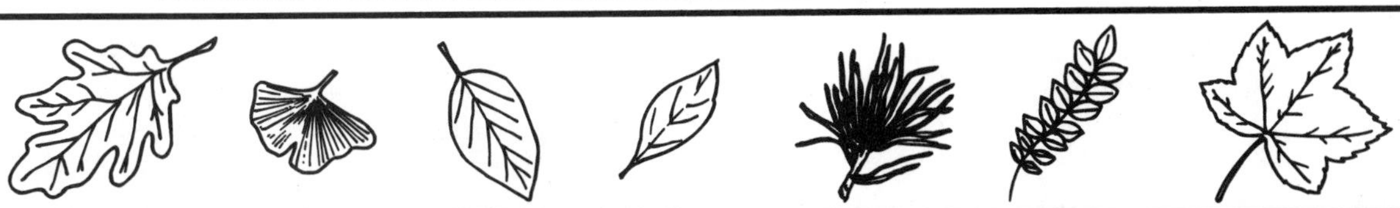

_____

Plant Interview Sheet

Write your answers under the questions.
Write your own question for question 5.
Your partner will use these questions to
interview you in front of the class.

Question 1: What type of plant
are you?

_____

_____

Question 2: Where do you grow?

_____

_____

Question 3: Do you produce chlorophyll?

_____

Question 4: What is your most unusual
feature?

_____

_____

_____

Question 5:

_____

_____

_____

Fairy Ring Reports

Materials:
"Mushroom and Fairy Patterns" (p. 38), "Super-Duper Fact Card" on mushrooms (p. 73), scissors, pens or pencils, crayons

Directions:
1. Duplicate a copy of the "Mushroom and Fairy Patterns" for each child.
2. Have children research mushrooms using the "Super-Duper Fact Card" or other resource materials. They can review mushrooms in general, or choose specific mushrooms to study (see list below).
3. Have the children write their favorite fact or facts on the front of the mushroom patterns.
4. Let children decorate the mushrooms with crayons.
5. Post the completed mushroom reports on a bulletin board, making a circular fairy ring from the patterns.

Option:
Let children decorate the fairy patterns and post them above the mushrooms.

Types of Mushrooms:
• Bird's Nest
• Cauliflower Mushroom
• Golden Chanterelle
• Chicken-of-the-Woods
• Destroying Angel
• Earthstar
• Elves' Saddle
• Fly Agaric Mushroom
• Honey Mushroom
• Inky Cap

Peculiar Plants! © 1998 Monday Morning Books, Inc.

Mushrom and Fairy Patterns

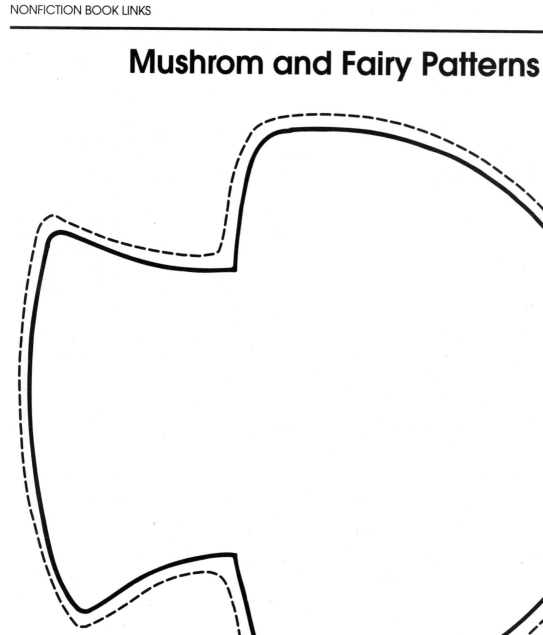

Learning About Leaves

Do this activity several times during the year: in autumn (with leaves that change color), in winter (with evergreen leaves), and in spring, when the new leaves are growing.

Materials:
"Learning About Leaves" Hands-on Handout (p. 40), "Leaf Observation Sheet" Hands-on Handout (p. 41), leaves, crayons or markers, scissors

Directions:
1. Duplicate a copy of the "Learning About Leaves" and the "Leaf Observation Sheet" Hands-on Handouts for each child.
2. Bring in leaves for children to observe. Collect them from trees in your area, or ask children to bring in leaves they find.
3. Have children observe the leaves and compare them to the "Learning About Leaves" Hands-on Handout. They can look for the stem, veins, pores on the surface of the leaves, and so on.
4. Have the children record their observations on the "Leaf Observation Sheet."
5. Collect the sheets and keep them for comparison later in the year, after children have done the activity again.

Options:
• After observing the collected leaves, use books to identify which trees the leaves are from. Seal the leaves between two sheets of clear Contac paper and cut them out. Use thread to suspend them from a hanger to make leaf mobiles. Attach paper labels to the thread labeling each type of leaf.
• Place the leaves beneath thin sheets of paper and provide crayons for children to use to make rubbings.

Learning About Leaves

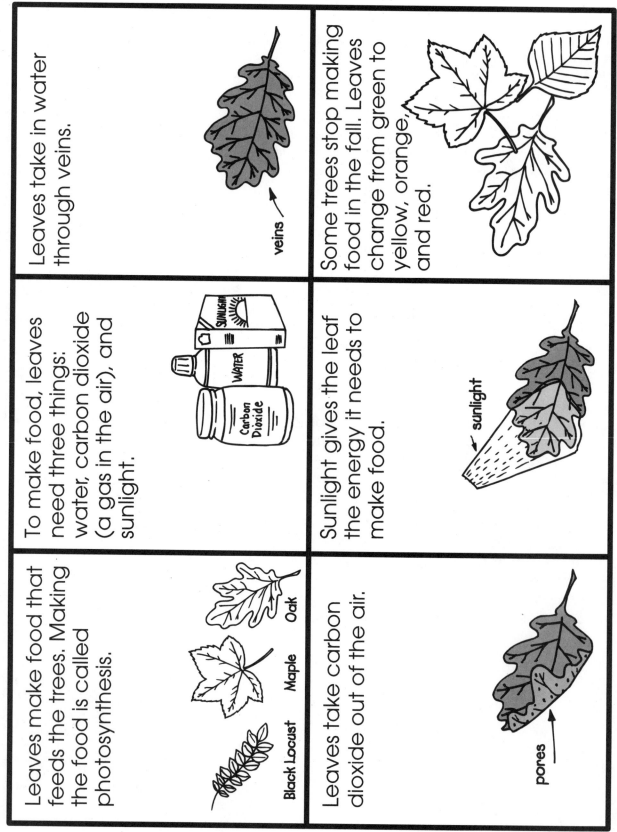

Leaves take in water through veins.

veins →

Some trees stop making food in the fall. Leaves change from green to yellow, orange, and red.

To make food, leaves need three things: water, carbon dioxide (a gas in the air), and sunlight.

SUNLIGHT

WATER

Carbon Dioxide

Sunlight gives the leaf the energy it needs to make food.

← sunlight

Leaves make food that feeds the trees. Making the food is called photosynthesis.

Oak

Maple

Black Locust

Leaves take carbon dioxide out of the air.

pores →

Leaf Observation Sheet

My name is ...

- My name is: _____

- The date is: _____

- The season is (circle one): fall, winter, spring, summer

- This is my leaf. (Draw a picture, or make a rubbing of your leaf.)

(Label the veins of your leaf. Label the stem.)

- My leaf is colored _____.

- If you know what type of leaf you have, label it.

Camouflage Report

Plants help a variety of animals to hide from predators. Algae on sloths help them blend with leaves. Orchid mantises blend in with white orchids. Walking stick bugs look like twigs. Dead-leaf mantises look like leaves. Lions blend with golden grasses.

Materials:
"Camouflaged Critters" Hands-on Handout (p. 43), books on camouflage (see list below), crayons or markers, scissors, large sheets of paper, tape

Directions:
1. Duplicate the "Camouflaged Critters" Hands-on Handout for each child. Enlarge patterns, if necessary.
2. Have the children research animals that use camouflage. Provide books on camouflage for children, or let children use the Hands-on Handout.
3. Children can cut out one of the animals on the Hands-on Handout, or draw their own animal.
4. Have children write one fact upside-down on the back of their animals. (When the animals are lifted from the background, the facts will be right-side up.)
5. Provide art materials for children to use to draw backgrounds for their animals to blend into.
6. Help children attach their animal patterns to their backgrounds using a hinge of tape so the animals can be lifted and the facts read.

Camouflage Books:
• *Animal Camouflage: A Closer Look* by Joyce Powzyk (Bradbury, 1990).
• *Hide and Seek*, edited by Jennifer Coldrey and Karen Goldie-Morrison (G. P. Putnam's Sons, 1986).
• *How Animals Hide* by Robert McClung (National Geographic Society, 1973).
• *How to Hide a Polar Bear and Other Mammals* by Ruth Heller (Grosset & Dunlap, 1985).

Camouflaged Critters

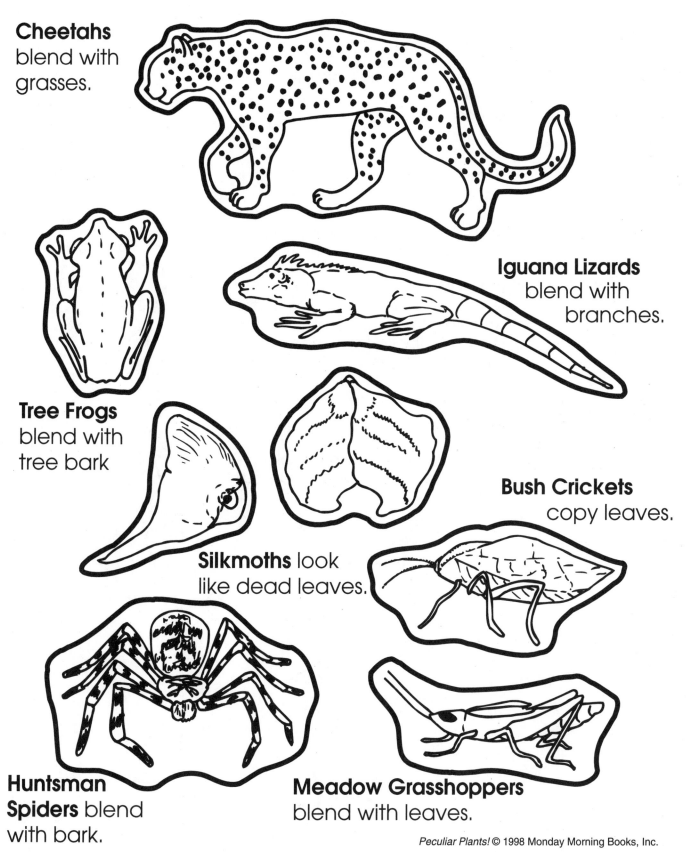

Cheetahs blend with grasses.

Iguana Lizards blend with branches.

Tree Frogs blend with tree bark

Silkmoths look like dead leaves.

Bush Crickets copy leaves.

Huntsman Spiders blend with bark.

Meadow Grasshoppers blend with leaves.

Peculiar Plants! © 1998 Monday Morning Books, Inc.

Fact Tree Forest

Materials:
"Leaf Patterns" (p. 45); "Super-Duper Fact Card" on bottle trees (p. 70), eucalyptus trees (p. 71), mangrove trees (p. 72), palm trees (p. 73) and sequoia trees (p. 75); scissors; pens or pencils; crayons; brown construction paper; tape or glue

Directions:
1. Duplicate a copy of the "Leaf Patterns" for each child.
2. Divide the class into groups of four or five. Have the children choose trees to research. They can review trees in general, or choose specific trees. Children might want to study trees that grow in their area.
3. Have children research trees using the "Super-Duper Fact Cards" or other resource materials.
4. Have each child write a fact on one of the "Leaf Patterns."
5. Let each group make a tree. They can create a trunk using brown construction paper and other art materials. Then they can attach the fact leaves to the trees.
6. Post the completed tree reports together on a bulletin board to make a forest of fact trees.

Option:
Children can research and draw the type of animals or insects that live in their trees. They can attach the animals to the fact trees.

Leaf Patterns

45

The Secret Garden

Story:

The Secret Garden by Frances Hodgson Burnett, illustrated by Tasha Tudor (J. B. Lippincott, 1912, 1968).
An orphaned little girl named Mary is sent to live with her uncle in a house on the Yorkshire moors. Here, she discovers two secrets: an invalid boy who is kept in his room and an abandoned garden. The garden, and her friendship, help the boy to regain his health.

Setting the Stage:

• Find England on a map or globe with the children.
• Take a field trip to a botanical garden, or visit a pretty garden in your town or neighborhood.
• Show children pictures of different flowers from a garden magazine.
• Plant a garden at your school, or plant a window box in your classroom.
• Bring in different floral-scented perfumes for children to smell and try to guess which flowers are in them.

Tricky Tongue Twister:

• *Some spy knows a super special secret.*

Peculiar Plants! © 1998 Monday Morning Books, Inc.

My Secret Garden

Materials:
Manila file folders (one per child), writing paper, crayons or markers, glue or tape

Directions:
1. After reading aloud *My Secret Garden*, ask the children to close their eyes and imagine their own private gardens.
2. Have them picture what a perfect hideaway would mean to them.
3. Give each child a sheet of writing paper and have the children write a description of their own secret gardens.
4. Give each child a file folder. Have the children glue their stories inside the file folders on the left-hand side.
5. Provide crayons and markers for the children to use to draw their secret gardens on the right-hand sides of the file folders.
6. Have children decorate the fronts of the folders to look like closed gates.
7. Children can write "My Secret Garden," or another heading, on the front of the folders.

Option:
Make folders by folding large sheets of construction paper in half.

Miss Rumphius

Story:

Miss Rumphius by Barbara Cooney (Viking, 1982).
In this beautifully illustrated storybook, Miss Rumphius is the Lupine Lady. In order to make the world a better place, she travels the land planting the seeds of the blue and purple lupine flowers. Wherever she travels, her flowers remain.

Setting the Stage:

• If possible, bring in an example of lupine flowers for children to observe and smell.
• Let children plant flower seeds in your playground. Or contact your City Hall and see if your class can begin a city beautification program, planting flower seeds in unexpected areas.
• Show famous pictures of flowers, such as Monet's water lilies.
• Bring in a bouquet of wildflowers for children to draw. Provide construction paper and charcoals or pastels for children to use to draw still lifes.

Tricky Tongue Twister:

• *Lovely lupine lasts a long time.*

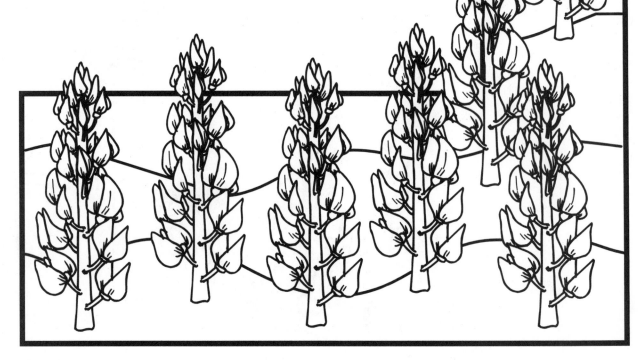

Flower Power

Materials:
"Flower Pattern" (p. 50), pencils, colored construction paper, scissors, green yarn, tape or glue

Directions:
1. Divide the children into groups of five.
2. Duplicate the "Flower Pattern" and cut out. Use this pattern as a template to make a flower for each group of children. (Make the flowers from colored construction paper, or let children do this.)
3. Give each group a writing prompt from the list below. Or let children write one or two sentences describing the book *Miss Rumphius.*
4. Each child will take one petal and finish the writing prompt.
5. Transcribe the writing prompt and the children's names in the center of the flower.
6. Assemble the flowers and post on a "Flower Power" bulletin board. Use green yarn to make stems for the flowers.

Writing Prompts:
• My favorite flowers are _____, because....
• One way to make the world a prettier place is....
• I would/would not like to travel the world, because....
• Miss Rumphius was known as the Lupine Lady. I would like to be known as _____, because....

Option:
Children could write a fact on each petal. They could choose their facts from the books listed in the Nonfiction Resources.

Note:
If your class is not divisible by five, you can add petals to one flower, or make one flower with fewer petals.

Tricky Tongue Twister:
• *Fragrant flowers flourish after showers.*

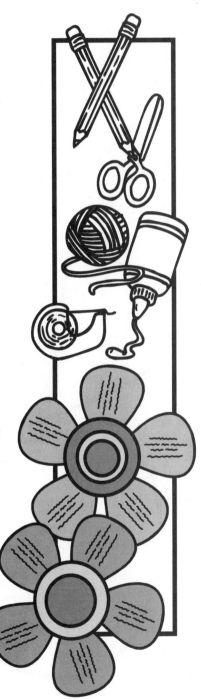

Peculiar Plants! © 1998 Monday Morning Books, Inc.

Flower Pattern

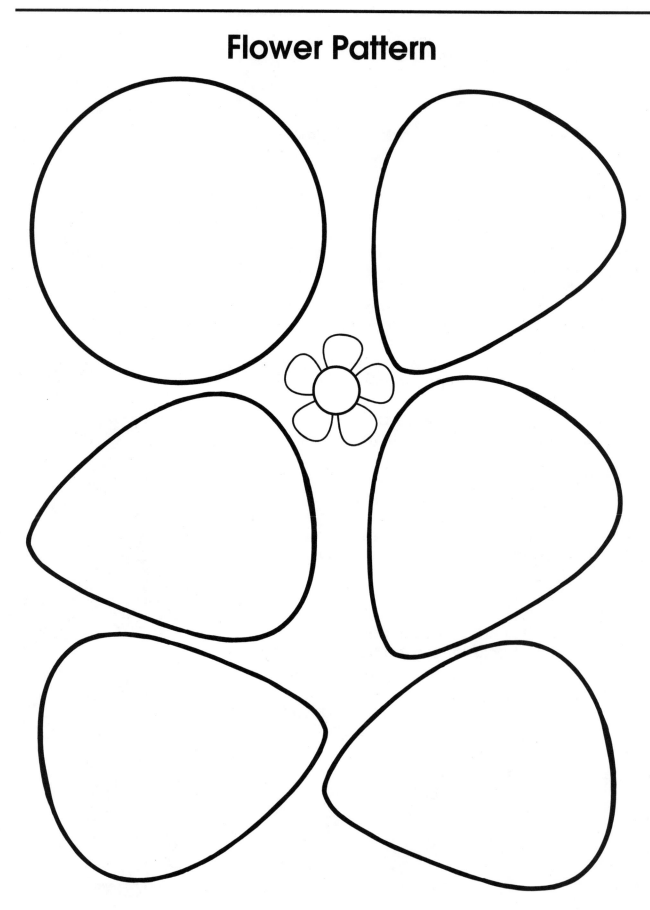

Carrie Hepple's Garden

Jack-in-the-Pulpit

Story:

Carrie Hepple's Garden by Ruth Craft and Irene Haas (Atheneum, 1979).
A group of children in search of a ball that went over the fence venture into the magical, mystical garden of Carrie Hepple. Although they are afraid of the old woman, who seems so frightening to the youngsters, they are won over by the delightful curiosities in her garden.

Setting the Stage:

• Read this book to the children outside, on a sunny day.
• *Carrie Hepple's Garden* is told in rhyme. Share other rhyming books with the children, such as the ones listed below.
• Provide watercolors and watercolor paper for children to use to create their own versions of Carrie Hepple's lovely garden.
• Discuss the flower "Love-in-a-mist," and discuss other plants that have equally descriptive names, for example:

      crab's eye (also called rosary pea)
      angel wings (also called elephant ear)
      Queen Anne's Lace
      Jack-in-the-Pulpit
      horsetails
      Indian paintbrush

Indian paintbrush

Rhyming Books:

• *Let's Marry Said the Cherry* by N. M. Bodecker (Atheneum, 1974). (The title poem lists many fruits and vegetables.)
• *When We Were Very Young* by A. A. Milne (Dell, 1924). ("Daffodowndilly" is a unique description of a flower.)
• *Where the Sidewalk Ends* by Shel Silverstein (Harper and Row, 1974). ("The Garden" is a beautiful poem.)

Crab's eye

Peculiar Plants! © 1998 Monday Morning Books, Inc.

Rhyme Time

Materials:
Writing paper, pencils

Directions:
1. After reading *Carrie Hepple's Garden*, challenge the students to create plant rhymes of their own.
2. Write the names of a variety of plants on the board (refer to the "Plant A to Z List" on page 77).
3. Have the children brainstorm rhyming words. Start them off with the following examples:

• flower:	power	shower	glower	hour
• rose:	nose	toes	chose	hose
• tree:	free	me	see	bee
• fruit:	suit	flute	boot	lute

Remind children that the flower, tree, or plant does not necessarily have to be the word that is rhymed. Colors, or other descriptive words, are sometimes easier to find rhymes for. For example:

• green:	seen	mean
• blue:	true	you
• red:	head	sled
• pink:	think	wink

4. Have children string together simple rhymes. For example:

She smelled the rose with her nose.

More advanced students can take the rhymes further:

She smelled the rose with her nose,
Then watered it with a green hose.
The rose that she chose,
Was open, not closed,
And as pink as the paint on her toes.

The Garden of Abdul Gasazi

Story:

The Garden of Abdul Gasazi by Chris Van Allsburg (Houghton Mifflin, 1979).

A young boy named Alan is left in charge of a mischievous dog named Fritz. During their afternoon walk, Fritz leads Alan into the mysterious gated garden of the retired magician Abdul Gasazi. Amazing things happen in this garden, and by the end of the day Alan is not sure whether he believes in magic or not.

Setting the Stage:

• Take children on a field trip to a botanical garden. Or show pictures of famous gardens, such as Monet's garden at Giverny (see list below).

• Bring several flowering plants into the classroom and create your own indoor garden.

• Spread a sheet of butcher paper on the floor and provide children with colorful tempera paints. Have them paint a beautiful flowering garden. Post this as a backdrop in your classroom.

• Put on a magic show. Check out books on magic tricks from the library. Host a magic show for younger grades or for parents.

Books on Monet's Garden:

• *A Blue Butterfly: A Story About Claude Monet* by Bijou Le Tord (Doubleday, 1995).

• *Linnea in Monet's Garden* by Christina Bjork, drawings by Lina Anderson (Rabén & Sjögren, 1985).

Books on Magic:

• *Be a Magician! How to Put on a Magic Show and Mystify Your Friends* by Jay Boyar (Julian Messner, 1981).

• *Magic Across the Table* by Bill Severn (David McKay, 1973). Also by the author: *Magic Shows You Can Give, Magic Wherever You Are*, and *Shadow Magic*.

Tricky Tongue Twister:

• *Don't be tricked by the tropical topiary.*

Peculiar Plants! © 1998 Monday Morning Books, Inc.

Make a Topiary

Materials:
Thin cardboard, cookie cutters, scissors, green construction paper or felt, markers, Popsicle sticks, glue, small paper cups, dirt

Directions:
1. Show children the cover of *The Garden of Abdul Gasazi*.
2. Explain that a topiary garden is one in which live trees and shrubs have been clipped to look like animals or birds or other decorative shapes.
3. Give each child a thin piece of cardboard.
4. Set out cookie cutters for children to trace.
5. Help children cut out their shapes.
6. Have each child glue a Popsicle stick to one side of each cookie cutter shape.
7. Provide green construction paper, felt, or other material for children to use to cover their cookie cutter shapes.
8. Give each child a small paper cup filled with dirt.
9. Children can stand their topiary animals in the cups.
10. Display the topiary shapes.

Option:
Provide ribbons and other materials for children to use to decorate their topiary animals.

Marvelous Mother Goose

Story:
There are several Mother Goose rhymes that feature plants. Duplicate the sheet of rhymes for your students. Then work together to create marvelous Mother Goose sachets.

Setting the Stage:
• Bring in several of the herbs and flowers mentioned in the rhymes for children to smell: lavender, parsley, sage, rosemary, thyme.
• In October, carve a pumpkin for your classroom. Give each child orange, green, and black construction paper to make their own Halloween jack-o'-lanterns. Check out the book *From Seed to Jack-o'-lantern* by Hannah Lyons Johnson (Lothrop, 1974).
• Have children guess what flower the first poem is about. (It's about a daffodil.)
• With the children, try to make up more riddles about different flowers or plants. They can also try to create plant-themed tongue twisters.

Plant Riddles:
• What planet doesn't the fly want to visit?
      Venus! (A Venus flytrap)
• What kind of a man lives in saltwater?
      A mangrove tree.
• What kind of moon grows in your backyard?
      A moonflower.

Tricky Tongue Twister:
• *Mother Goose's gardener grows great green grapes.*

Peculiar Plants! © 1998 Monday Morning Books, Inc.

Mother Goose Rhymes

Daffy-Down-Dilly
Daffy-Down-Dilly has come up to town,
In a yellow petticoat and a green gown.

Mary, Mary, Quite Contrary
Mary, Mary, quite contrary,
How does your garden grow?
With silver bells and cockle shells,
And pretty maids all in a row.

Lavender's Blue, Diddle, Diddle
Lavender's blue, diddle, diddle,
Lavender's green:
When I am king, diddle, diddle,
You shall be queen.

Can You Make Me a Cambric Shirt?
Can you make me a cambric shirt?
Parsley, sage, rosemary, and thyme.
Without any seam or needlework?
And you shall be a true love of mine.

June Brings Tulips
June brings tulips, lilies, roses,
Fills the children's hands with posies.

The Rose Is Red
The rose is red, the violet's blue,
The honey's sweet, and so are you.

A Ring, a Ring o' Roses
A ring, a ring o' roses,
A pocket full of posies,
Ashes! Ashes!
We all fall down!

I Had a Little Nut Tree
I had a little nut tree,
Nothing would it bear.
But a silver nutmeg and a golden pear.

Mother Goose Sachets

Materials:
Mother Goose Rhymes (p. 56), thin colored paper (origami paper works well), tape or stapler, dried herbs or flowers (as fragrant as possible) in small dishes, shredded paper scraps, scissors, glue

Directions:
1. Give each child two sheets of thin colored paper.
2. Have children place one sheet of paper on top of the other, and then tape or staple three sides of the square closed.
3. Have children choose their favorite Mother Goose rhyme to cut out and glue to the front of their sachets.
4. Provide assorted herbs for children to choose from.
5. Have children stuff their sachets with assorted herbs and flowers, plus shredded paper.
6. Help children seal the open end of their sachets.
7. Children can give the sachets as gifts.

Option:
Let children write their own rhymes, sayings, slogans, riddles, and so on to put on their sachets.

Mother Goose Book Link:
• *My Very First Mother Goose*, edited by Iona Opie, illustrated by Rosemary Wells (Candlewick, 1996).

Chrysanthemum

Story:

Chrysanthemum by Kevin Henkes (Greenwillow, 1991). Chrysanthemum is a mouse who loves her name. Until she enters school, that is, and the other children make fun of her. Each day, Chrysanthemum feels worse about her long name. Then a wonderful music teacher, whose name is Delphinium Twinkle, arrives and saves the day!

Setting the Stage:

• Bring in a name book (see list below), and read children the different histories of their names. If a child's name is not in the book, ask the child to find out why his or her parents chose the name.

• Have children share times when they felt uncomfortable, the way Chrysanthemum feels during parts of this book.

• Brainstorm other plants and flowers that are used as names, and see if children can think of books they've read in which the names were used. For example:

> Tulip (in Rosemary Wells' *Benjamin and Tulip*)
> Lilly (in Kevin Henkes' *Julius, The Baby of the World*)
> Violet (in Roald Dahl's *Charlie and the Chocolate Factory*)

Name Books:

• *Baby Names from Around the World* by Maxine Fields (Pocket Books, 1985).

• *The Best Baby Name Book* by Bruce Lansky (Meadowbrook, 1984).

• *The Baby Name Countdown* by Janet Schwegel (Paragon House, 1990).

Tricky Tongue Twister:

• *Delphinium Twinkle's a star to her students.*

People-Plant Book

Materials:
Drawing paper, crayons or markers, pens or pencils, hole punch, brads

Directions:
1. Give each child a sheet of paper and have the children fold the papers in half.
2. Have children draw self-portraits on one half of the papers and write one or two sentences about their names.
3. On the other half of the papers, have children draw themselves as their favorite plants. They can write the name of the plant below the picture, and then blend the name with their own. For example, if a child named Melanie wanted to be a cactus, she might write: Melacactus.
4. Bind the completed pages in a People-Plant Book.

Options:
• Have children write one fact about their chosen plant on the plant-half of their pages.
• Have each child draw a picture of himself or herself as a plant. Post the plants on a "Classroom Garden" bulletin board.

Jack and the Beanstalk

Story:

When poor Jack and his mother run out of money, Jack takes the family cow to the village to sell. Along the way, a trickster convinces Jack to trade his cow for three "magic" beans. Jack's mother, upset with the trade, throws the beans out the window where they take root and grow into a magic beanstalk. In the morning, Jack sees the beanstalk and climbs into the sky, where he meets a giant. Brave Jack steals the giant's gold, a goose that lays golden eggs, and a harp. Jack quickly climbs down the beanstalk and chops it in two before the giant can follow.

Setting the Stage:

• Spray-paint poker chips gold for coins and plastic eggs for golden eggs. (Do this without the children present.)
• Give each child a clear plastic cup, a damp paper towel, and three beans. Have students place their beans in the cup with the crumpled damp towel. Discuss what the beans will need to sprout (sunlight and, eventually, soil and water). Consult a book on growing beans, such as *Beans: All About Them*, by Alvin and Virginia Silverstein, illustrated by Shirley Chan (Prentice-Hall, 1975).
• Let children make paper bag giants. They can stuff large paper grocery bags with newspaper scraps and then paint "giant" features on the front of the bags.

Jack and the Beanstalk Versions:

• *Idle Jack* by Anthony Maitland (Farrar, Strauss, 1977).
• *Jack and the Beanstalk* by Steven Kellogg (Scholastic, 1965).
• *Jack and the Giant Killer: Jack's First and Finest Adventure Retold in Verse as Well as Other Useful Information about Giants* by Beatrice de Regniers (Atheneum, 1987).
• *The Jack Tales: Told by R. M. Ward and His Kin* by Richard Chase (Houghton Mifflin, 1943).

Writing a Retold Tale

Materials:
"Writing a Retold Tale" Hands-on Handout (p. 62), writing paper, pens or pencils, scissors, crayons

Directions:
1. Discuss the fact that sometimes writers create new versions of famous stories, for example, Raymond Briggs' *Jim and the Beanstalk*.
2. Provide several retold tales (see list below) for children to read. Or read the stories to the class.
3. Duplicate a copy of the "Writing a Retold Tale" Hands-on Handout for each child.
4. Go over the directions on page 62 with the students, and write a sample story together as a class. Then challenge the children to create their own retold tales.
5. Cut out simple leaf shapes from writing paper. Children can write the final drafts of their tales on the leaf shapes.
6. Post the finished stories on a large green yarn "beanstalk" growing up the wall of the classroom.

Options:
• Younger children can dictate their stories.
• Students can work together in teams to create cooperative tales.

Other Retold Tales to Share:
• *The Frog Prince Continued* by Jon Scieszka, paintings by Steve Johnson (Viking, 1991).
• *Jim and the Beanstalk* by Raymond Briggs (Coward, McCann, 1970).
• *Max and Ruby's First Greek Myth* by Rosemary Wells (Dial, 1993).
• *Max and Ruby's Midas: Another Greek Myth* by Rosemary Wells (Dial, 1995).
• *The True Story of the 3 Little Pigs by A. Wolf* as told to Jon Scieszka, illustrated by Lane Smith (Viking, 1989).
• *The Stinky Cheese Man and Other Fairly Stupid Tales* by Jon Scieszka, illustrated by Lane Smith (Viking, 1992). This is a Caldecott Honor Book.

Writing a Retold Tale

What You Do:

1. Choose a tale you'd like to rewrite.

2. Think about the most important things that happen in the story. These are called "plot points." In "Jack and the Beanstalk," the plot points are:
- Jack sells his cow for beans.
- Jack's mom throws the beans out the window.
- The beans become a magic beanstalk.
- Jack climbs the beanstalk.
- Jack takes the giant's treasure.
- Jack cuts down the beanstalk.

In your tale, you will want to keep most of the story the same, but change a few plot points. For example, if you were writing about "Jack and the Beanstalk," you might make the giant nice. Then Jack wouldn't steal from him, but instead might invite him to dinner. All the other plot points stay the same.

3. Next, think about the characters. You might change the main character to a girl. If you were writing a new version of "The Three Little Pigs," you might change the pigs to some other animal.

4. Once you've decided what plot points will be different and what will be the same, you're ready to write your story. Make sure to tell the story in your own words!

From: Jack
To: Mr. Giant

You are invited to a dinner party at my house.
Jack

You are invited to...

Peculiar Plants! © 1998 Monday Morning Books, Inc.

Peculiar Plants Program

Songs:
- Oh, Give Me a Rose
- Hybrid Roses
- An Evergreen's Leaves
- Evergreen, Evergreen
- Plants That Eat Insects
- Hello, Mr. Fly
- I'm a Little Glow Plant
- Avocado Song
- Flytrap Rap

Featuring:

Oh, Give Me a Rose

(to the tune of "Home on the Range")

Oh, give me a rose
I can smell with my nose,
One that blooms in the garden so bright.
Roses blossom each day
When I walk by this way.
There are red ones and pink ones and white!

Their scent is so grand.
I stop in the yard and I stand
Just to smell their perfume.
I'll bring one to my room.
It's the best flower scent in the land!

Hybrid Roses

(to the tune of "Take Me Out to the Ball Game")

There's a rose that's named Gypsy.
There's a rose that's named Peace.
There's a rose known as the Matterhorn,
One that's called Friendship,
       and one called Popcorn.

There's a rose named for Cinderella.
There's Hula Girl and Pascali.
But the one that I love the best
       was named after me!

Note: Children can wear rose masks made from paper plates and colored construction paper. Attach the masks by punching holes at the sides and threading through with yarn.

An Evergreen's Leaves

(to the tune of "My Bonny Lies Over the Ocean")

An evergreen's leaves don't change color,
Their thin, narrow leaves withstand cold.
They keep their leaves all through the winter,
Now and then losing the old, the old.

Evergreen, evergreen,
Your leaves will never turn brown, turn brown.
Evergreen, evergreen,
Your leaves will never turn brown.

Evergreen, Evergreen

(to the tune of "Jingle Bells")

Evergreen, evergreen,
Your leaves don't turn brown.
Even in the autumn,
Your leaves don't fall down.

Myrtles, pines, and spruces,
Holly trees and firs.
Other trees lose leaves,
But you keep all of yours.

Note: Children can wear simple costumes made from
paper grocery bags and painted with green tempera.
Real leaves can be glued to the bags, as well.

Peculiar Plants! © 1998 Monday Morning Books, Inc.

Plants That Eat Insects

(to the tune of "Take Me Out to the Ball Game")

There are plants that eat insects.
There are plants that eat meat.
They trap their prey with a juice that sticks.
When an ant steps on it, oh, what a trick!

There are sundews and Venus flytraps,
Bladderworts, pitchers, and jugs,
And they all want one thing to eat:
All those yummy bugs!

Hello, Mr. Fly

(to the tune of "Home on the Range")

Hello, Mr. Fly,
Wouldn't you like to try
Some sweet nectar I've made just for you.
Just take a sip, and try hard not to slip,
Down the slick inside walls of my tube.

One slip of your feet,
Will give me a yummy fly treat.
Uh oh, there you go,
Yes, you fell down below.
And that's how a pitcher plant eats.

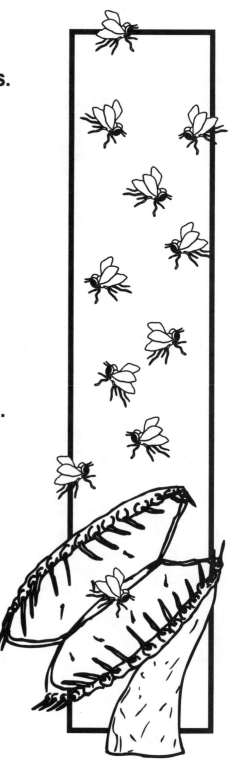

I'm a Little Glow Plant

(to the tune of "I'm a Little Teapot")

I'm a little glow plant.
I shine bright.
You can see my colors,
Late at night.
My light's like an orange-yellow spark.
If you want to see me,
Wait 'til dark.

Note: Glow plants are fungi. Children can wear paper plate hats for the fungi caps. Punch holes in the plates and thread through with yarn for ties. Decorate with glow-in-the-dark paint.

Avocado Song

(to the tune of "Clementine")

Avocado, avocado, avocados,
Black or brown.
With a yellow-green flesh inside,
And a pit that's sort of round.

Avocado, avocado, avocados
Are not new.
They've been found in tombs
    with mummies,
In the country of Peru.

Avocado, avocado,
Named by Aztecs long ago.
You can find them in your grocery,
But they came from Mexico.

Note: Children can paint paper grocery bags green for avocado costumes.

Peculiar Plants! © 1998 Monday Morning Books, Inc.

Flytrap Rap

I like bugs,
'Cause they're good to eat.
I trap crawling ants,
And a fly's a treat!

I trap bugs.
I've got many tricks.
I've got slippery walls,
And a juice that sticks.

So come on, bugs,
Come on, ants and flies,
Just come visit me,
For a big surprise!

Flies
Welcome!

Peculiar Plants! © 1998 Monday Morning Books, Inc.

Algae

Habitat: Algae usually grows in water. All seaweeds are algae.
Colors: Algae comes in different colors: green, brown, red, and blue-green.
Food Source: Algae provides food for many sea creatures.
Camouflage: Small creatures often hide in sea algae.

Super-Duper Fact: Algae are primitive plants. They don't have true roots, stems, or leaves.

Avocado

Habitat: Avocados grow in the U.S. and Latin America.
Appearance: Avocados are pear-shaped. The most common type has bumpy black or brown skin with yellow-green flesh.
Names and Nicknames: "Avocado" comes from an Aztec word. Avocados are also called alligator pears.
Uses: Avocados are used as food, in body creams, and in Latin America are given as wedding gifts.
Super-Duper Fact: Avocado seeds have been found buried with Peruvian mummies dating back to 750 B.C.

Bamboo

Habitat: Bamboo grows in warm climates.

Way of Growing: New bamboo plants grow from seeds or from shoots that sprout from stalks underground.

Size: Some bamboo plants grow as high as 120 ft./37 m. and have stems that are 1 ft./30 cm. in diameter.

Flowers: Bamboo plants rarely bloom, and usually die after they bloom.

Uses: Bamboo is used to make fishing poles, baskets, cooking utensils, and other products. Bamboo can be eaten as a vegetable. Pandas eat bamboo.

Super-Duper Fact: Some types of bamboo can grow 36 in./ 91 cm. in 24 hours.

Bottle Tree

Habitat: Bottle trees grow in dry areas in Australia.

Appearance: The main part of the trunk is short and thick. Just below the branches, the trunk narrows. This makes the trunk look like a round bottle.

Size: The trees grow as tall as 60 ft./18 m.

Water: Bottle trees store water under their inner bark.

Relatives: Bottle trees are related to the Baobab tree found in Africa.

Super-Duper Fact: The inside of the tree is made of soft, spongy material. This material contains jelly-like sap.

Eelgrass

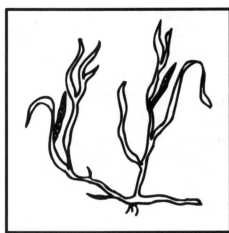

Habitat: Marine eelgrass grows in muddy, shallow bays along the Atlantic and Pacific coasts of North America. It roots on the ocean floor. It bears slender, floating stems. Freshwater eelgrass grows in ponds.
Colors: When eelgrass is alive, its leaves are bright green. When dead, eelgrass turns black.
Plant Type: Eelgrass is not a seaweed or algae, but a true flowering plant.
Food Source: Marine eelgrass is eaten by wild ducks and geese.
Nicknames: Freshwater eelgrass is also called tape grass and wild celery.
Super-Duper Fact: Eelgrass flowers are pollinated underwater.

Eucalyptus

Habitat: Eucalyptus trees can be found in Australia and North America.
Tree Type: Eucalyptus trees are evergreens.
Size: Eucalyptus species are among the tallest trees known. One type of eucalyptus grows to a height of over 300 ft. (91 m.).
Food Source: Koalas depend on eucalyptus leaves to survive.
Nicknames: Eucalyptus trees are also called ironbark, bloodwood, and gum tree.
Super-Duper Fact: Koalas remain bug-free because they eat eucalyptus leaves. The leaves give their fur a smell bugs don't like.

Mangrove Tree

Habitat: Mangrove trees grow along tropical coasts. They live at the edge of the ocean in shallow water.
Appearance: Mangroves have odd-looking prop roots that are smooth and slippery.
Way of Growing: A mangrove's roots start above the water, grow sideways in the air, and then curve down through the water into the mud.
Names and Nicknames: Mangrove trees are called "the trees that walk."
Super-Duper Fact: When a new tree starts to grow, it can grow one inch (2.5 cm) every hour!

Moonflower

Habitat: Moonflowers grow in warm or hot climates.
Relatives: The moonflower is related to the morning glory.
Appearance: The moonflower is a climbing vine. It has broad, heart-shaped leaves.
Flowers: Its white flowers are shaped like trumpets.
Size: This vine can grow to 30 ft./9 m. high. The flowers may be 3 to 5 in./8 to 15 cm. across.
Fragrance: The flowers have a very strong smell.
Super-Duper Fact: Moonflowers open at night and close in the sunlight.

Mushroom

Habitat: Mushrooms grow on trees, leaves, and in grasses.
Size: Mushrooms can be very tiny or giant. Cauliflower Mushrooms can grow to 50 lbs./23 kg.
Type of Plant: Mushrooms are fungi.
Seeds: Mushrooms do not have seeds. They grow from spores.
Dangerous: Some mushrooms are very poisonous. Poisonous mushrooms are sometimes called toadstools.
Super-Duper Fact: A painting of a mushroom was found in the tomb of Pharoah Amenemhep dating from about 1450 B.C.

Palm

Habitat: Palm trees grown in warm climates.
Food Source: Coconut and date palms provide food and other products.
Size: The coco palm tree can grow to 100 ft./30 m. tall.
Type of Tree: Palm trees are called broadleaf evergreens.
Seeds: One type of palm tree has a seed that can weigh 45 lbs./20 kg.
Super-Duper Fact: Palm oil, which is made from the fruit of the coconut palm, is used in soap, candles, margarine, and other products.

Poison Ivy

Habitat: Poison ivy can be found in Southern Canada and in the U.S.
Relative: Poison ivy is related to poison oak.
Color: The leaves of poison ivy are red in the early spring. Later, they change to shiny green. In the fall, the leaves turn red or orange.
Leaves: Each leaf is made up of three leaflets. The leaflets have notched edges.
Itchy Business: Poison ivy contains poisonous oils that can get on a person if a plant touches any part of the body.
Super-Duper Fact: You can get poison ivy by touching an animal that has walked through a patch.

Pussy Willow

Habitat: Pussy willows grow wild in the eastern part of North America.
Size: Pussy willows grow to be about 20 ft./6 m.
Appearance: Pussy willows have branches with several long, straight twigs. On the twigs, there are many flower buds.
Relative: Pussy willows are related to weeping willows.
Buds: Pussy willow buds are soft and fuzzy. They look like tiny kittens climbing up the twigs, and are called catkins. A scale protects the bud from the cold. In warm weather, the bud scales fall off.
Super-Duper Fact: Pussy willow pollen is very lightweight. The slightest breeze carries it far.

Saguaro Cactus

Habitat: Saguaro cacti live in the Arizona desert.
Size: These cacti can grow to be higher than a two-story building.
Water: Saguaro cacti have long roots. The roots soak up water when it rains. Sometimes the cacti drink so much, they burst!
Housing: Birds build nests in hollowed-out holes in the cactus. After the birds leave, a desert mouse might move in.
Flowers: Birds, bats, and insects drink the nectar from the cactus' flowers.
Super-Duper Fact: Saguaros can live for over 100 years.

Sequoia Tree

Habitat: Today, sequoia trees grow naturally only in California.
Size: Sequoias are the largest living trees in the world. They can grow to be 250 ft./76 m. tall, with 30 ft./9 m. wide trunks.
Age: Sequoias can live for over 2,000 years.
Leaves: Sequoia leaves are short and prickly.
Type of Tree: Sequoias are conifers, plants that have cones. Sequoias make 2,000 new cones each year. They are evergreens.
Super-Duper Fact: Some sequoias weigh 10 times more than the female blue whale.

Venus Flytrap

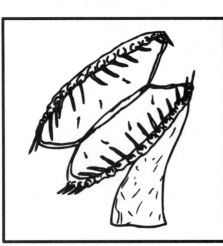

Habitat: Venus flytraps are found only in the swamps of North Carolina.
Food: Flytraps eat insects and spiders.
Size: The plants can grow to be 1 ft./30 cm. tall.
Flowers: In the spring, white flowers bloom on top of tall stalks.
Leaves: Narrow leaves grow in a circle around the plant's base. Each leaf opens into two halves, attached in the center. On the leaves' surface are trigger hairs.

Super-Duper Fact: If a bug crawls onto the open leaf's surface, it disturbs the trigger hairs. The leaf halves quickly close.

Sunflower

Habitat: Sunflowers originally grew in North America. They were brought to Europe in the 1500s.
Size: Sunflowers can grow from 3 to 10 ft./1 to 3 m. tall. The flower head can be more than 1 ft./30 cm. in diameter.
Flowers: A sunflower can have one or more heads of flowers.
Seeds: One sunflower can produce 1,000 seeds.

Uses: The seeds are rich in protein. Sunflower oil is used to make margarine and cooking oil. The seeds are used in birdseed.
Super-Duper Fact: The sunflower's head turns and faces the sun throughout the day.

Plant A to Z List

A: Acacia, Algae
B: Banyans, Bladderworts
C: Chicken-of-the-Woods (mushroom)
D: Dandelions, Daphne, Deciduous Trees,
E: Evergreen Trees,
F: Fungi
G: Ginkos
H: Herbs, Hibiscus, Hydrangea
I: Ivy
J: Japanese Maples, Jonquil
K: Krubi
L: Lichens, Lily-of-the-Valley, Lotus, Lupine
M: Mangrove, Marigolds, Moonflowers
N: Narcissus
O: Orchids
P: Pitcher Plant, Pumpkin, Pussy Willow
Q: Queen Anne's Lace
R: Rose, Rhubarb
S: Saguaros, Scotch Brooms, Sundews
T: Thistle, Thyme, Tomato
V: Venus Flytraps, Violet
W: Wisteria
Y: Yew, Yuccas
Z: Zelkova trees

Peculiar Plants! © 1998 Monday Morning Books, Inc.

Playdough Recipe

Ingredients:
4 cups (1 kg) flour
2 cups (.5 kg) salt
8 tsp. (40 g) cream of tartar
10 tsp. (50 ml) liquid vegetable oil
4 cups (1 l) boiling water
food coloring (in desired colors)

Directions:
1. Combine the first four ingredients in a large bowl.
2. Add food coloring to the boiling water.
3. Pour the water into the dry ingredients and mix.
4. Remove the dough from the bowl and knead on a floured surface.

Note:
Be careful when adding the boiling water if children are around.

Nonfiction Resources

- *Carnivorous Plants* by Cynthia Overbeck, photographs by Kiyoshi Shimizu (Lerner, 1982).
- *Discovering Trees* by Jill Bailey (Bookwright Press, 1989).
- *Fairy Rings and Other Mushrooms* by Gladys Conklin, illustrated by Howard Berelson (Holiday House, 1973).
- *From Flower to Fruit* by Anne Ophelia Dowden (Thomas Y. Crowell, 1984).
- *Giant Sequoia Trees* by Ginger Wadsworth, photographs by Frank Staub (Lerner, 1995).
- *Growing Colors* by Bruce McMillan (Lothrop, 1988).
- *How Leaves Change* by Sylvia A. Johnson, photographs by Yuko Sato (Lerner, 1986).
- *How Seeds Travel* by Cynthia Overbeck, photographs by Shabo Hani (Lerner, 1982).
- *Mushrooms* by Millicent E. Selsam, photographs by Jerome Wexler (William Morrow, 1986).
- *My First Nature Book* by Angela Wilkes (Knopf, 1990).
- *The 100-Year-Old Cactus* by Anita Holmes, illustrated by Carol Lerner (Four Winds Press, 1983).
- *Plant Experiments* by Vera Webster (Children's Press, 1982).
- *Plants Do Amazing Things* by Hedda Nussbaum, illustrated by Joe Mathieu (Random House, 1977).
- *Plants That Eat Animals* by Linna Bentley, illustrated by Colin Threadgall (McGraw-Hill, 1969).
- *Plants That Never Bloom* by Ruth Heller (Grosset & Dunlap, 1984).
- *The Plants We Eat* by Millicent E. Selsam (William Morrow, 1981).
- *Poisonous Plants* by Suzanne M. Coil, illustrated by Astrid M. Lenox (Franklin Watts, 1991).
- *Pollinating a Flower* by Paul Bennett (Thomas Learning, 1994).
- *Seeds* by Terry Jennings (Gloucester, 1988).
- *Sunflower* by Martha McKeen Welch (Dodd, 1980).
- *Vegetables* by Susan Wake (Carolrhoda, 1990).
- *Wildflowers Around the World* by Elaine Landau (Franklin Watts, 1991).
- *Wonderful Pussy Willows* by Jerome Wexler (Dutton, 1992).
- *Your First Garden Book* by Marc Brown (Little, Brown, 1981).

Web Site Addresses

Botanical Garden Web Sites
• Royal Botanic Gardens Sydney
http://www.visitorsguide.aust.com/~tourism/sydney/
attracts/botanic/gardens.html

Carnivorous Plant Web Sites
• Bladderwort
http://www.mos.org/sln/sem/wort.html
• Carnivorous Plants
http://www.paonline.com/pub/USER/m/mrmiller/main.htm
• Venus Flytraps
http://scholar3.lib.vt.edu/cp/Droseraceae/dionaea.html

Fungi Web Sites
• Edible and Poisonous Mushrooms
http://www.state.mo.us/conservation/nathis/flora/mushroom
/mushroom.html

Rose Web Sites
• The Virtual Rose Garden
http://www.pathfinder.com/@@zyOxWQQAYw@V65rU/
vg/Gardens/NYBG/Gardens/modern.html

Saguaro Cactus Sites
• Saguaro Cactus
http://www.opus1.com/emol/tour/tucsaguaros.html
• Saguaro Cactus photo
http://www.goldcanyon.com/htm/cac_rock.htm

• The best efforts have been made to find current Web sites. However, Web sites sometimes change. In addition to using these sites, also try keyword searches, such as gardens or specific plant names.

Note:
The fungi page should be used for pictures and information ONLY. Do not pick wild mushrooms with children!